monika herceg
initial coordinates

COPYRIGHT © 2018, 2022
Monika Herceg

ENGLISH TRANSLATION © 2022
Marina Veverec

DESIGN & LAYOUT
Nikša Eršek

PUBLISHED BY
Sandorf Passage
South Portland, Maine, United States
IMPRINT OF
Sandorf
Severinska 30, Zagreb, Croatia
sandorfpassage.org

Originally published by SKUD
Ivan Goran Kovačić as *Početne koordinate*.

COVER ART
Danijel Žeželj

PRINTED BY
Znanje, Zagreb

Sandorf Passage books are available to the
trade through Independent Publishers Group: ipgbook.
com / (800) 888-4741.

Library of Congress Control Number: 2021952098

ISBN 978-9-53351-372-0

This book is published with financial support by
the Republic of Croatia's Ministry of Culture and Media.

monika herceg

initial coordinates

TRANSLATED FROM THE CROATIAN BY
Marina Veverec

SAN-
DORF
PAS-
SAGE   SOUTH PORTLAND | MAINE

With gratitude to the editors of the following
publications in which these poems first appeared:
"early autumn," "full circle," "curses," "inheritable
traits," "fertility," "tiny deaths," and "same old
stories," *Poetry International Web*; "harvest" and
"pampering," *Denver Quarterly*; "thunder god," "deaf
cats," "snake deaths," and "birth defects," *Harvard
Review*; "bird deaths," *Exchanges*; "infectious diseases,"
"lake," "ouroboros," "respading," and "fruit,"
Asymptote; "pants" and "late autumn," *Verseville*;
"escape," "withering," "inheritable diseases,"
"grandma's eye," "rabbit deaths," and "the water had
long escaped before the violence," *Exchanges*.

contents

with caution we step beyond the tree line
aware below our feet lies
intact death
a path but a few can pass
a journey to the family tree

we remember to watch for salamanders
a step on them deafens
we remember to let the snakes pass
should they cross our path
for they engulf all creatures cunningly
just like the morning thickens
the milk of early mists
contaminating all foothills and notches

the moles hidden within the burrows
perfect the softness of the clay
the forest's rib bones bulge
on warmer days
then jab the unwary hikers
as if about to cough out
the rose hip and humidity

waking up
in the bed of autumn
our soles are hot
our body stabbed by the beeches' ribs
we always bud out
as the sun's jaw tightens
round the bareness of the forest

snake deaths
(origin)

early autumn

the dripping beeches' souls creak at night
their rings expanding like ripples on the water
starting point of the world and the north
a concentric circle

cyclamens sense
somnolence seeping in bolder
eroding the bulbs
as it settles on their fertility

herons move september
from one side of the lake to the other
following the sun sliced in reeds
as loud women are washing the clothes
knee-deep in ice-cold water
cracking open like spiny husks of chestnuts

only one thing left to do
to plow through the depth of dream once more
share the remaining light with deer
who strip their furs before twilight
to warm the hands of women

harvest

grandma goes first and with a dowsing rod
slender and long
shakes the trees
back hurts from lengthy gathering
we squat then stand and stand
and squat with sticky fingers
not seeing
that the baskets
covered in the purple skin of summer
have been pushed to the part of the earth's orbit
muffled by the sound of ripening
unaware of how
the presence of worms irreversibly eats away
the seams of september

from the very moment of the drop everything awaits the
boil

deep barrels will boil
with purple heat
childhood and the brittle bones of august
the whole orchard will boil that stranded toil
of the forthcoming autumn
smelling
of plum dumplings

full circle

the analogy of body decay
and autumn decay
is total
the leaves humbly submit themselves to rot
we stick our fingers into the flesh
feeling for the pulse of summer
in the apples we're storing in the basement
long after it they will abide the chill
stinging the tissue
and then like a planet
enter the eternal orbit around the winter

pickling peppers and cucumbers
preserves the sense of a full circle
the pickled sun essence
lightens the stomach

past the winter jars
sometimes snakes pass sluggish
their skins thick and green
grandma says they're already tame
underneath the house
ever since the basement was built
they sleep as guards
hibernating like us
with solar flares
in their abdominal cavities

thunder god

my grandmother's mother hauls water from the stream
and sleeps
among the leaves when no one is looking
as a young woman she fell arm-first
into a cauldron of lard
and a big scar covered
her entire forearm

she would always speak of
her children
six sons and one daughter
sprouting up like mushrooms
summer after summer
back in those fertile rainy years

on a long past july afternoon
the thunder god hurled a bolt
straight at their barn
cats lost their ears
her sons
scattered like ants
to the other side of the equator

pampering

grandma often used to say
her actual father was
mato from the neighboring village
who carries travels tucked under his hat
like rose hip carries its seeds
and visits them as soon as
the last bark goes silent

their teeth-hollowing poverty
he was burying with loam and pushed down
among the bones of the fallen stock
just like the rough fat hands of her mother
full of acorns and hazelnuts
the quails convinced they are women

at times he would stop and light a cigarette
at the crossing of the village road
letting the birds and bees
completely cover him
in a cloud of smoke

he collected kernels of rotten fruits
left behind after harvests
having faith in the healthy core
and now it doesn't matter
from which side the winter comes
as there is nothing left to do
but to dig and delve
the necessary pampering of the soil
after a tedious summer

gatherers

once the chestnut yields the woods are packed with
gatherers
their voices run through the women's backs
like wild animals
rejuvenating them with foreign accents
and opening their plump bodies
like empty closets

leaving their shoes and good intentions in the woods
foreigners come running barefoot to the beds
creasing the dry skin
under their fingertips like under the frost eyes crack
like grape berries right before ripening
and instead of roosters awaken the village

in the early summer children sprout in the vineyards
fatherless
like mushrooms after the rains

deaf cats

when the thunder god rearranged the sky
the first lightning struck our barn
and the second struck young kata

they buried her neck-deep
in the garden next to the onion beds
and waited two days
for her arms to sprout
out of the wet black soil

it was yet another miracle
the villagers had witnessed
our deaf cats meowing wretchedly
not hearing their own voices
nor the purring guts full of mice and kittens
and kata wore the lightning underneath her heart
now skipping
like a broken toy

snake deaths

my grandmother's youngest brother
long lay face-down in the hay
before they discovered
his young corpse

when the walnuts peered out of their green pods
he gathered their wrinkly heads
cracked them bare then ground them
the sunday gibanica cake smelled
of homecoming

in the early evening they put
a bullet in his dome
dragging him back down
to the center of the earth

adders kept vigil over him
like points of a compass
so quartering the death
that slept in him

growth

they were cutting the trees like pigs
and at times it seemed more blood would spill out
from an oak severed from the soil
than from a pig hung upside down
for the rest of death
to drip out

they chopped the root branching down to packages
hiding the diseases
and noise pollution in the soil

we've seen
chimneys perforating the clouds' guts
a city spreading out like tuberculosis
a directionless wind we couldn't spell out
a growth impossible to wall off

when grandma married she was an old maid
the ironworks had already evolved into a complex being
feeding all its children
and her long hundredfold arms
crawled along by the bellies of trains
disentangled across the world

trains

when the first train passed
it seemed to the villagers the night was a candle
lit up and blown out
as the loud engine pleased
and nothing here'd ever remain
holy and silent

only kata loved the noisy caterpillars of metal
she'd put the sheep and cows out to pasture
by the rails on tuesdays
then obediently observe them
conversing with god

curses

grandfather married
into hectares and hectares of mixed forest
the same amount of arable land
a few orchards and vineyards
four horses
a dozen cows goats hens rabbits
a barn bigger than the house
and grandma was plump and healthy
ruddy as apples and overripe tomatoes

word around the village was she had not yet married
for she was a big mouth
not to let the estate go under
she first taught her husband
the things that bring the greatest evil
to kill a snake at the doorstep
or banish the gypsies
it can do no harm to be cautious not to clip nails
on fridays sundays and tuesdays

he soon took to drinking
grandma says he wasn't wary
of putting his right foot first on the ground
and putting on the right shoe
he would leave early to catch a train to ironworks
and return in the dead of the night
always with a few miniatures of bitters
that soothed his growing ulcers
and grandma would cuss him out
for instead of the hundreds of liters
of homemade rakija
he drinks the store-purchased ones

inevitability

gypsy women always come before the first snow
as if they divine the darkening
pushing itself out of the premature smothering of
autumn
the valley's wooden back breaking
under the weighty body of the wind as unnoticed
as metamorphosis of cramped grubs to cockchafers
the disturbed ground pushes against the steps
while dispersing earthworms out of its cheeks
on late autumn days
the sky at once brims with evening
and the tiny maledictions dive into the eyes
unexpected like gnats

it is said one should let them cross the threshold
and host them
or else they cast curses upon offspring
neighbor's wife conceived three times
and each time lost the fruit
after they banished a gypsy woman

to thin out the witchcraft
grandma puts garlic at the bed's edge
she has also planted a birch
right outside the window
when the first swarm of light enters the birch's bones
we clearly hear
the inevitable blooming
the invisible fingers
of the curses caught
knocking against the pane

premonition

the winter returns as the thick
sheet of fog spreads across the ravaged gardens
still wrapped in a dream we seldom sense a footstep
quiet like the fox's slink into the henhouse
or gaining wisdom

inhaling and exhaling the endless miles of night
the cold matures
into the first morning frost
now the plains are killing fields mopped around
by rain-drenched ghosts
of undug tubers
potatoes and beets

fatigue evaporates out of the frozen furrows
sooner and sooner
keeping watch over them like a worried mother
soon all will lie down in the darkness that
sooths the pains of growth

bird deaths
(escape)

silence

piety of snow
envelops the village in layers
like a cabbage head
the conversion of thoughts to words happens
depending on the temperature of air
and often two tongues
exchange nothing
but the silence
unnaturally smooth and warm
its dreg long urging a cough

as long as there's ember in the hearth
women are sitting
knitting socks
and mumbling on the lord's prayer

god responds
with orion's reapers' trembles
too soft for them to hear

hunt

the night grows out of the foxes' backbones
detaching from the soaked body
subtle as the spin of the earth
their snouts strung tight as slingshots
the air clanking the whiskers
as though the wind is shaking off the stars
into the deep whiteness

before sunrise hunters tramp the snow down to the tree
stand
then patiently for hours on end
set their eyes in sights
like sprained ankles

the winter morning broke out with deaths
like autumn with red berries

out of the open wounds
the mute ghosts of roosters
raise their heads like antennae
and let out voiceless crows
until they drip off
into the opacity of the fog

inheritable traits

while beneath the surface
stillness strengthens the roots
that will provide the growth
by the furnace grandpa puffs the rings of smoke
says like a prophet this winter
shall be the fiercest of all
but even the winter is tame inside
by the fire
where cats lazily purr
furs clean of friskiness

when he dozes off by the furnace
he often dreams of electric trains
the aging still ahead of him
the baldness unnoticed grows
in the middle of his scalp
like a glade
unborn descendants lose their hair
and have a weak heart
closing the circle
of inheritable traits

birth defects

sometimes women bloom
amidst the greatest snowstorms
so the neighbor anka helped deliver my father
on the dirt floor by the hearth
the snow already knee-deep

as a child he pursued animals
seeking in them
the hidden lumps of solitude
buds that overgrew his own throat too

he didn't like being around people

when he was five
an enraged swarm of hornets
swooped down on him
from the den of a hop hornbeam
he cried out his sting-swollen eyes
and then without a blink
continued his hiding game in the tree hollows
rearranging the piles of soil
not noticing
his soles expanding and lengthening
the first mustache cropping up
until he tripped over his own foot
as if over a molehill

bird deaths

no one speaks of birds
in whom the winter settles
the light hardens on their feathers
so they drop from the frozen clouds
feeble and full of landscape

winter corrodes the sparrows' most insistent
inner waymarks
so they plummet through the sky like
kamikaze
into piles of white peace

for generations we have kept the secret
that birds do not die indeed

with the first southern wind
the sunspots in them come alive
taking them back to initial
coordinates

amnesia

the warmth is borrowed from rakija
plums inhale the flavors of the sun
then the pomace brings to boil
the core of the summer heat
scattering twilight sooner than cockcrowing
onto the tree crowns
villagers have fire for supper
to peel off the film of darkness
the layers of melancholy on their organs
in the morning the north wind
bends the drunken necks

last night our neighbor searched for his brother
who died ten years ago
his brother's death clots in the corner of his mouth
every time rakija thins out
the ancestral murmur just under the skin

in every night there lies an abyss
still as a barn before the fire
a bitter summer sip is a necessity
so as not to retreat after once more
the fire-crazed bullocks come stampeding through

infectious diseases

ljuba withered abruptly
in a few weeks her fat arms
deflated like bagpipes
first came the doctors then village gypsies
but no one could grasp
where the winter entered her bloodstream
so as to squeeze out the venom
only her eyes remained big
the two glass marbles
that dissected fears like a prism

when she entirely transformed into a spore
they threw her frozen eyes
to the bottom of the lake swelling like dough
in the spring months
for the rusalka nymphs to thaw out the inevitability of
disease
underneath the malnourished ribs

lake

coming home from the village's barrelhouse
mato fell into a ditch drunk
and slumbered in the snow

meridians of his travelogues
fell out of his hat
and sunk into the depths of the soft snow
drawing on the icy cushion
a unique map of the world
four continents on which
he drove wild horses
sprang up underneath the dry snow
volga's delta slopped over
right under his head
and he dreamt of the fishermen
in the caspian sea
throwing the nets
filling them with rare specimens
gigantic belugas and sterlets
carelessly awakening
the creatures petrified at the bottom

the largest lake
mato always told the neighbors
its waters never flow out

he never married
had children
nor grandchildren
and had he
maybe he would've run faster and bolder
like startled cattle

when the water snakes surfaced
and dragged him down
to the bottom

goblins

if a winter is cold enough
the village dogs freeze and their scrawny bodies
for months seem like museum specimens
if an icy wind blows
their tails fall off
so they stand there maimed

on such winters a pack of wolves
descends from the mountains
as dogs will not sell them out
on such winters
goblins in heaths multiply
and enter villagers like a seasonal flu

grandma says it's always been like that
the goblins crawl inside the mouth when you least
expect it
then after midnight visit the wolf dens
the wolf children grow in the wombs of women

we mustn't be deceived says grandma
by the children's faces they put on
wolves in them grow faster than humans
and sooner or later
they shall bite

heads

the deep snow is harder on the hunters than the gatherers
their deft feet crossing forest slopes
pushing ahead as if possessed
by the need to find a prey
in vain
the whiteness dazzles their senses too
and the tracks of the game are but dead-end loops

that same night they dreamt without a care
of the southerly wind
that had melted the snow

first they came for the hunters

their heads
still full of sunny meadows
they set
around the village
like streetlamps

ouroboros

grandma fed them warm leftovers of the moon
stored in the basement alongside apples
and once their teeth came in
unexpected like the first snowfall
they let us run off
before the transformation was complete

i was a newborn when they carried me
through labyrinths of beech limbs
astray
we seemed a family of rabbits
and when any of us would cry
the forest's bare bodies stifled
the density of the sobs

they could smell us
freezing with suspense

they could hear the wood hardness
ripening in our lungs

along the way we planted stories in the hawthorn shrubs
so the offspring could find their way back
and in that earth's spin
we would've become half-trees
had the unhealthy warm east wind
not swept
the last of our traces
and finally blew in
the spring

fertility

the precise strikes of the hoe
crack the winter out of the fields
the days ripen into cherries
women into tough stalks

mother's care is as rough as the tongue of a cat
long it enfolds and cleans the soil from pests
licks the fur of straying animals
cleaning them off the bad habit of entering the yard
out of her arms sprout the seedlings of cabbage and
radish
she then replants into the throats of billets
out of her knees grow the greenest chards
mother's skin is covered in sprouts instead of in hairs

before noon she always lays down
along the bluest bone of the sky
then with a belly full of early light
rams the morning into her womb
and grafts
the long necks of fertility
onto tiresome trees

in vain
in our house
wherever it may be
live people who died

the spring never comes in

cat deaths
(exile)

brother

as a child he caught polio   45
so they kept tossing him into the ice-cold water
to quench his blazing organs
but only upon taking a breath he truly burned
as if he'd absorbed the nuclear processes of the stars

maybe later saint anthony jumped in
when god didn't feel like it
so brother walked despite the three other diseases they
discovered
in his spongy skeleton

he was raising unnamed birds in his head
talking to them more often than to people

there'd been one more thing the fiery sun corona left
underneath his too green skin
so that sometimes
when no one is looking
he glows in the dark

wooden arm

mother's arm had swollen
like a damp limb of a beech
and woodened
out of its dry crepe skin
came out forest demons
if they'd cut it off she wouldn't have had enough
tenderness
to bring up two children

brother once pulled a pot full of ants over his head
the worry made her tree bark fall off
and made her grow a third a tenth
a hundredth arm
for each ant

burnt arm

they transplanted skin off his leg to his arm
inch by square inch
to cover the raw open wound flesh
and we'd come to the hospital for months
bringing cookies and juice

working at brickyard father
molded building blocks
to bring warmth to other families
to our home he brought
a burnt arm once
a busted head four times

on that early afternoon
they came and told us they're rushing to the hospital
and i kept repeating the entire thing
should be cooled under running water
recalling what they once did
when i burned my arm
leaning it against the furnace

arm in nettles

mother often put nettles in her stew
neighbors would always look at her weird
when she'd pick through the grass and look for
fetticus dandelion and nettles
stretching their necks and bending their backs
right next to our yard
behind the fence

mother said only young ones are fit for eating
they grow more spiteful and grouchier with age
not forgiving a touch

some young nettles even lied next to her plate
to scare us
if we nagged about not wanting to eat

when we would come to him in tears
father put his arm among their elongated necks
and let them bite him like thousands of mosquitoes
and then called us
covered in red blisters
the children of medicinal herbs

locomotives

brother liked to climb old locomotives
his eyes grow larger the second he sees them
standing there full of shortened distances
letting the rust spread across them unnoticed

they had eaten enough
wistful looks and greetings
departures
arrivals
everyday worlds
for their lasting to be equal to
the snap of a camera
we were careful to wrap
the unobtrusive landscape of the station
into a moment
my mother's back as she's holding my brother
not to slip from the wheel
his broad smile of two teeth
my finger pointed at the passersby

it missed nothing
except maybe mother's worry
that cannot be captured
from behind

dot

in grandfather's stories
the fiery locomotive mouths
engulf the awakening of the hills
as he commutes to work
still yawning

we fear their blaze
but sympathize
so making up adventures
we bring the beat back to the tracks
watching for hours
how the distant rails
merge into a dot

blackberries

as august arrives we gather blackberries
along the neglected railroad
minding we step
from tie to tie
in between lies the abyss
that ends the game
i am the master of walking on trails
i put one foot in front of the other
careful as a wire-walker

even though nothing remains of the tracks
but the untaken journeys
meandering through hills
we imagine what it'd be like
if a train passed right now
and we jumped in

we'd send a postcard
from a sunnier region
one that could fit an entire happy family
into one june
like a hearty sunday meal
fits on a small plate

tiny deaths

unbearable sultriness urges loud breaths
sleeping in the same room
angst heavier than the air
fills out the space like carbon dioxide
and we suffocate in the nightmare

in father's dream emptiness proliferates
like potato bugs
until they've completely destroyed the crops
at times he coughs
like a cat trying to cough up
a ball of fur
brother grinds his teeth
mother is motionless
her lips pressed
alike our lady's in the painting she prays to
now and then i lean over her face
to check if she's breathing

i listen and
as we are outgrowing our already tight shoes
as our hair is growing darker
and our cartilage erodes as we run
the atmosphere outside combusts
and the child in us burns
like birthday candles
so rapid that in the morning we
do not remember

cat deaths

for weeks observing the passing planes
my brother figured cats too could fly
he threw them as high as he could
then ran to mom yelling
look it flies
they always landed on their feet
except once old mickey
belly-first dropped by chance
on the edge of a stump

a few days later
greeted us at the threshold
his lifeless grey-furred body
as dignified
as the dead mice
he would bring
to our doorstep

math compass in hand

i stretched out my palm for ten switch strikes
i lie saying i didn't know what i've done wrong
a monster stabbing a math compass
into her brother's hand
we are seven combined
and we speak a made-up language
like the one when peaches
communicate through the sun between their fuzz
of all this we are
in the summer comprised of short shadows
in the winter cocooned in blankets

after each strike I sigh
but never cry
the hand pulls itself away in fear when lashed
by the smooth willow switch

we are only seven combined
and when no one is looking
we glow in the dark

pants

the first dead man i ever saw
was my uncle
shaved and his hair parted left
handsome like my ken
his ear was pierced
i can't remember which one
but before the funeral they took his earring off
uncovered only his head
and upper torso
we could see his tie
and the seam of his shirt
said they didn't bother dressing the rest
as the body was smashed
in the accident
he so departed without the other half of the suit
wheresoever one is to travel
down the piles of sticky loam

mother long dreamt
of his stiff face
and when father had died
she didn't open the casket
nor let us look at him
before the burial

big dog

after uncle's funeral
i saw the bright august sky
open up
and the tears of saint lawrence
entered the mouths of the deceased
then rose them
like lanterns
up to the summer constellations

that same winter we buried mimi
at the back of our house
and grandfather later showed me
where to find her
opening the bellies
of the dead stars
in which she might've
built a den

barrel

those years i kept having the same dream
i'm running back to our house hoping i'd make it
just in time for us to flee
neighbor points me to the forest
says they won't go after me
the forest reeks of rakija
at times it's enough to hide in the basement
for their broad shoulders can't pass
and i'm still tiny enough
to squeeze through the ground holes
or vanish in an oak barrel

everything reeks of rakija
and i refuse to believe in a god
i can't talk to
as i'm biting my nails trapped inside the barrel
as i'm catching my breath running through the forest
as i'm digging tunnels
holding fireflies in my mouth
beneath our house

same old stories

grandma and grandpa live in the next-door room
before bedtime i crawl into their bed
and intently listen

the story always gets caught on the undergrowth
struggling like chestnut harvesters
through the muddy forest paths
beaten by the tracks of wild game
once again grandma speaks
of when drunk grandpa took the horses to town
and returned without them
of her brother who died during
a long-forgotten war
of a house whose wood evolved into bricks

it's already getting dark
and the stories close along with eyelids
depriving the words of visual effects
the scent of freshly cut grass rushes in through the duvet
the mooing of thirsty cows out of the pillow

a fictitious dog is barking outside the window
as grandpa is coming

by foot

without the horse

words

on hot summer days
grandpa would sit for hours
under the walnut tree in our backyard
piling his old age into sighs
precisely measuring
the pressure pushing july against his face
when the swelter would start dizzying the head
peeking through the door grandma would yell
to get away from the sun
she always carried a handkerchief for it was proper
and wiped the sweat off her forehead
as if collecting the rain before a drought

she believes god helped once in the hospital when
fever was turning brother blue as a plum
he might've helped once more
when she'd forgotten what was in her words
and god would not let her depart
before the others had read them

dream book

when we misbehave
mother scares us

grey-furred sharp-teethed
bristly scraggy
famished
bloody-muzzled
rabid wolves
will come for us

i drench my bed
in sweat and urine
in my nightmares
their teeth are falling out
and mother says
it can only mean
someone is certainly
to die
again

rabbit deaths
(return)

respading

my mother visits the cemetery once a year
not wanting the villagers to think we've
neglected the dead
she then arranges billets with care
heather saffron horsetail
and respades the graves as if it were
autumn hoeing of the garden
one is not to step on the toes of the dead

as under the ground an army of tiny creatures
disseminates limitless decay
feeling apathy and shame seems inevitable
to this fact that sadness fades
at the same pace death within them grows
unpleasantly rapid

hands

his hands shook as he smoked cigarettes
it was terrible in there so we avoided
to look into the empty room behind the eyes
in which he still might've sat
but we could no longer enter

father came with a switch

the first time
the second
the third
i hid behind grandpa's back
and he'd spread his arms like a big oak crown
with a thousand glowing words that calmed
every beast drawing near

escape

we started locking the room at night seeing
grandfather's shadow standing next to our beds
a knife in his hand
he said he heard footsteps around the house
and makes sure they don't drag us into the woods
for good

shortly after he spoke to the dead
for the first time
and fled leaping
the high fence of our yard
so the neighbors witnessed
four days later we found him
on the other side of town
hidden in a ditch

he said he was fleeing and must not return
someone's chopping off people's heads
and planting them in the woods
to grow an army

withering

he didn't get a chance to return with us
to live amongst vixens hedgehogs and does
but the image of orchard
he would give us as a gift every spring
with years flourished into a biosystem of his plums
his systematically rejuvenating big old pear
and the two cherry trees that would redden
always in may

amidst the autumn fusion
we would dig out a tunnel through time
and talk to him through death
overgrown with ivy
full of plum kernels
that nurtured us

once the withering took its turn
autumns ate themselves backward
no longer of our concern

no one picks plums
and grandfather sits alone
under the old pear
waiting for us to remember

inheritable diseases

a ring a spring another ring and a few coins
all of this they found in grandma's belly on the x-ray
we stared at the image and could not agree
whether insanity is inheritable or contagious

for years after she wouldn't come near us
she was a half-doe half-grandma
mud dripping off her hooves
we feared she would dirty us up
she would plant in us the seeds of autumn
that would overgrow us like weeds

saving the vows of my father
behind the belly button
she told me she had plenty of lads and deer
rumor has it they once found her
even with the priest
by the creek

grandma's eye

she laid full of dust
old maggoty furniture
of a renovated house
not recognizing us
and in a few weeks
she had wilted like a plant under snow
we could have carried her in our arms
along the entire circumference of the earth
so light almost woolen
but we waited for her to drain out
like juice out of the elderflowers
fearing the death that eats away from inside
slow enough to go unnoticed

at the beginning of february
mother found on her bed
only one frozen eye
the other one probably eaten by the cat
and let a whole bush of jasmine
grow out of it

fox

father had a few personalities he would change
depending on how much humidity was in the air
or autumn's depth
when the heavy october days
soaked his insides
he would sit on the porch
and call the stray cats
with a couple of swear words under his tongue
loosening miles far in the forest
on the spikes of chestnuts

when finer autumn days come
he lives in my mother's story and
if a sharp enough twilight
stretches along the edge of the forest
turns into a fox
and returns every ten years
as a curse

rabbit deaths

we stored death into animals with care
feeding them freshly cut grass and hay
and then drew the same death out of them painlessly
one incision under the neck

rabbit fur always hung from the old walnut tree
like an oversized coat
and next to the fur suit
the muscles we stripped bare
gazed at us in shame
and swayed in the gusts of wind

my father's stiff body mother
found by the rabbit hutch
one september morning
thus suspecting the axiom
we are rarely aware of

the death we feed to others
sometimes by chance
comes back into ourselves

bonding with death

father had died
all windows and doors are wide open
and if god passed through our house
we wouldn't even notice
the room is drafty

my hands are on my kidneys to keep them warm
these days when all the rooms are flooded
my fingers are pruned like walnut shells
my feet are in cold water for hours
and i pee all the time

my hair is wet
mother yells i'll catch a cold
but cannot close
the windows or the doors

bonding with soil

they should've
had more warm words to coat us
growing humans is hard labor
and mother's hands coarse and nescient

those days we tilled the soil for the corn competing
who'd be the first to finish the long rows
who'd be the first to burst into a butterfly
and fly off to the woods
blisters stuck out of our palms for days
and it was hard to heal properly
without the warmth

magic

magic moved in along with my mother

75
and the house walls overgrew with herbal recipes for
setting a family

neighbors turned into warlock mice
when we were somewhat older jozo moved in next door
his magnified mouse eyes
always glaring at us
behind the thick glass
at funerals mother would say
it's all because we are cursed
beneath our house
underground animals slither backward
and the twilight stretches our shadows
somewhat aslant

fruit

to break the curse
mother sacrificed a herd of sheep
a tractor chickens rabbits
she even let the corn die out

in january she blossomed for the fourth time
like a young cherry tree
the fruit had tiny eyes for good luck
and hair full of oak
half-doe half-sister

witch

apart from the signs appearing
as orderly wrinkles
around her eyes
nothing else tells of my mother's aging
everyone is below the ground
and for years her stories are a clod
a clod
clod
into the grave

at night she turns into a witch
taking a long ride through the neighbors' dreams

she steals their youth
her eyes still smiling like a child's
and she selflessly loves only the cats

mustache

at the end mother said
he had already tried a couple of times
to rip off the overripe fruits of rapture
and like them return to the hands of decay
in the attic
a noose around his neck
a month must've passed before she came out of her
room
after the funeral and it offered a kind of horrid solace
to her and to us
a humid oversaturation with grief
in every room
i still feel the thin lash of silence
stripping the space inside and outside of us
of its dignity
for there was nothing to say

she complains of backaches and his fists
somewhere in between her left and right ventricle
she still feels
his calloused heavy palms
and his thick mustache
like when he first married her

late autumn

the stillness of the forest is cleaved
by the unflinching drops of chestnuts
a sign the pellicle of an unobservable half-world
is permeable once more
the tree core is then carved
into the forest's memory
light wrapped into shorter days
deep breaths of november
impoverish the soil

the husking of summer
always stirs up the spirits
so they seep into the walls
like smoke into fabric

in every autumn dark comes after the dark
sharply and abruptly like wounding
begins the final hunt
death meeting us in person
before the doors close

the water had long escaped before the violence
into the cracks and faults of the earth's crust
so the forest lake had run dry

only one spring remained
from it drink wild boars and deer
and ghosts that wander
buckshot-packed

out of their heads
like out of acorns
grow a young forest

MARINA VEVEREC (1995) is a student of literary translation at the University of Zadar, Croatia, and occasionally a language editor at *[sic]*—a *Journal of Literature, Culture and Literary Translation*. Her translations have appeared or are forthcoming in *Denver Quarterly*, *Exchanges*, *Poetry International Web*, *Asymptote*, *Verseville* and *Harvard Review*.

She would like to express her gratitude to Tomislav Kuzmanović, Marta, Blaž, and A.M.

about sandorf passage

SANDORF PASSAGE publishes work that creates a prismatic perspective on what it means to live in a globalized world. It is a home to writing inspired by both conflict zones and the dangers of complacency. All Sandorf Passage titles share in common how the biggest and most important ideas are best explored in the most personal and intimate of spaces.